THE WILD WORLD OF ANIMALS

THE WILD WORLD OF ANIMALS

TIGERS

MARY HOFF

CREATIVE EDUCATION

Special thanks to Dr. Ronald Tilson, director of conservation for the Minnesota Zoo.

Published by Creative Education, 123 South Broad Street, Mankato, Minnesota 56001. Creative Education is an imprint of The Creative Company. Designed by Rita Marshall. Production design by The Design Lab.Photographs by Alamy (Westend61), Corbis (Theo Allofs, Tom Brakefield, Charles Philip Cangialosi, Pierre Colombel, John Conrad, Tim Davis, Martin Harvey; Gallo Images, Hulton-Deutsch Collection, Wayne Lawler; Ecoscene, Charles & Josette Lenars, Chris Lisle, Renee Lynn, Joe McDonald, David Muench, Naturfoto Honal, Reuters, Chase Swift, Randy Wells).

 Library of Congress Cataloging-in-Publication Data: Hoff, Mary King. Tigers / by Mary Hoff. p. cm. — (The wild world of animals). ISBN 1-58341-355-3. 1. Tigers—Juvenile literature. I. Title. II. Wild world of animals (Creative Education). QL737.C23H6188 2004. 599.756—dc22. 2004056162. First edition 9 8 7 6 5 4 3 2 1

It's dusk in Bandhavgarh National Forest in central India. Silently, a large, lanky tiger pads along the edge of the forest. Suddenly it stops, eyes and ears alerted by a movement nearby. Slowly, it creeps forward. Then it starts to run. It grabs its **prey**, a spotted deer, and digs its long claws into its flank. Its daggerlike teeth sink into the deer's neck. The animal struggles, then is still. The tiger drags its dinner to a sheltered spot in the woods and begins to eat. It's been a week since its last kill, and it is hungry.

Like house cats, tiger cubs are cute and playful **5**

KING OF CATS

Imagine a cat so big it could touch its nose to your bedroom ceiling if it stood on its hind legs. That's the tiger—the world's biggest wild cat. A male tiger can measure nine feet (2.7 m) from his nose to the tip of his tail. Some male tigers weigh 500 pounds (227 kg) or more. Females are smaller— usually about 300 pounds (136 kg).

Most tigers are orange with black stripes, but some are white with black stripes. Each tiger's stripe pattern is **unique** and helps provide **camouflage**. Orange tigers have white on their bellies and throats and on the insides of their legs. They also have a white spot on the back of each ear.

Tigers are the only wild cats with striped fur   **7**

Tigers are native to Asia. Until a century ago, there were eight kinds of tigers. Three—the Bali tiger, Javan tiger, and Caspian tiger—are now **extinct**. The remaining kinds are the Amur (Siberian) tiger, Bengal tiger, Indochinese tiger, South China tiger, and Sumatran tiger. The different kinds of tigers vary slightly in color, striping pattern, and size.

Bengal tigers can be orange or white **9**

Tigers live in many kinds of **habitats**.
Some live in northern **spruce** forests.
They have thick fur that protects them
from cold and snow. Others live in marshes
or swamps full of mangrove trees. Tigers
are good swimmers. Just like people, they
get into the water to cool off on hot days.
Because tigers live in many places, they
have many kinds of neighbors. Animals
that live near tigers include hyenas, monkeys, elk, and elephants.

Amur tigers live farther north than other kinds of tigers   **11**

Tigers are **carnivores** that use their big teeth and claws to help them catch their prey. Their teeth are good for biting and tearing. Their sharp, curved claws help them grab on to other animals. Tigers mainly eat wild deer, pigs, and wild cattle. A tiger may also eat monkeys and other small animals. On rare occasions, a tiger may kill and eat a human.

A tiger's teeth can be up to 3.5 inches (9 cm) long **13**

Sight and hearing are the senses a tiger uses most to find its food, even in the dark. A special structure at the back of its eyes helps a tiger see at night. A tiger can hear sounds that are much higher and much lower than the sounds a human can hear. Tigers use their sense of smell to keep track of other tigers.

Tigers can run very fast, but only for a short distance **15**

LIFE AS A TIGER

Daytime is naptime for a tiger. But as the sun sets, the tiger becomes more active. If it is hungry, it will begin to prowl in search of a meal. As it travels, it tries to stay out of sight in forests or tall grass.

Tigers capture prey animals by sneaking up on them and rushing in for the kill, or by waiting beside a trail and ambushing them as they walk by. After it catches a meal, a tiger may drag it to an out-of-the-way place before eating it. A tiger can eat 40 pounds (18 kg) or more of food at a time.

A tiger's stripes help it hide in tall grass as it hunts

In the northern part of their **range**, tigers mate in the winter. In the **equatorial** part of their range, they may mate any time of year. A little more than three months after mating, the mother tiger gives birth to two to four cubs in a sheltered place such as under a fallen tree or an overhanging rock. New tiger cubs weigh two to three pounds (0.9–1.4 kg). They have soft, striped fur,

18 Female tigers usually have cubs every two years

and their eyes are shut. The weakest cub often dies soon after birth.

Cubs remain with their mother for a year and a half to three years. At first, she feeds them milk. When they are two months old, she starts teaching them to hunt, and by the time they are a year and a half old, they can hunt on their own. In the wild, tigers live 10 to 15 years.

Male tigers do not help females raise the cubs **19**

Except for mothers and cubs, tigers live by themselves rather than in groups. Most tigers have a **territory**. A tiger lets other tigers know that a territory is taken by marking it with urine, scratch marks on trees, or scrapings on the ground. In places with lots of food, territories may be as small as 10 square miles (26 sq km). Where food is scarce, a single tiger may cover 400 square miles (1,036 sq km) of land.

Adult tigers communicate with each other in different ways. When they are close to each other, they make a quiet "chuff" sound through their noses. To communicate over long distances, they roar. You can hear a tiger roar two miles (3.2 km) away! Mothers and cubs communicate with quiet sounds. Tigers also growl, snarl, and make other noises.

Tigers and lions do not live near each other in the wild **21**

TIGERS AND HUMANS

Humans have long been in awe of tigers

because of their size, strength, and beauty.

The tiger is the national animal of India.

It is also one of the symbols of the Chinese

zodiac, which claims that people born

in certain years are like certain animals.

People born in the Year of the Tiger are

said to be powerful, confident leaders.

22   An Indian sculpture of a tiger and a woman

Tigers have often been featured in songs and plays. Many old Asian legends tell stories of encounters between people and tigers. *The Jungle Book*, a famous story by English author Rudyard Kipling, features a tiger named Shere Khan. Today, many things—from sports teams to computer programs—are named after tigers. People think this makes them sound powerful.

A tiger design in a stone walkway in China **23**

For centuries, traditional Asian medicine has used parts of tigers to heal and strengthen the body. Bones are said to help cure aching joints. Eyeballs are used to improve vision. Tails, whiskers, brains, blood, and other body parts have been used to treat brain disorders, laziness, toothaches, and more.

Early 20th-century tiger hunts involved large groups

Humans have hunted tigers since ancient times. Before guns were invented, people used nets, hidden pits, spears, and bows and arrows to kill tigers. Members of royal families in India used to hunt tigers for fun. In the 19th and 20th centuries, tiger hunting was a big sport. Some people hunted tigers to sell their parts for medicine. Over the years, tigers also have been killed because they have been seen as a threat to people and their livestock.

In the past, some countries tried to kill off tigers   **25**

People have also destroyed tigers' habitat, making it hard for them to find places to live. The remaining bits of habitat are often separated from each other, so tigers have a hard time finding each other to mate.

26   Tigers need large areas of land to survive

In recent years, tiger numbers have dropped so low that many people are concerned that the remaining tigers might die off and tigers will become extinct. A century ago, more than 100,000 tigers roamed the world. Today, there are about 5,000 to 7,500 tigers left in the wild.

Fortunately, many people are working to help tigers survive. The countries in which tigers live have made laws protecting the animals. They also have set up nature **reserves** for tigers. Many other countries have agreed not to allow people to sell tiger parts. If people continue to care about and protect tigers, these powerful cats will long remain part of our wild world.

30   Many people want to save these beautiful animals

GLOSSARY

Camouflage is coloring that helps make an animal hard to see in its surroundings.

Carnivores are living things that eat animals.

Equatorial means close to the equator.

An animal that is **extinct** can no longer be found alive anywhere on Earth.

The places where a creature lives are called its **habitats**.

The animals an animal eats are its **prey**.

The area of the world where a certain type of animal usually lives is its **range**.

Reserves are areas of land set aside to provide a place for animals to live.

Spruce is a kind of evergreen tree.

A **territory** is an area an animal claims for its own.

Something that is **unique** is one of a kind.

BOOKS

Markert, Jenny. *Tigers*. Chanhassen, Minn.: The Child's World, 1988.

Middleton, Don. *Tigers*. New York: The Rosen Publishing Group, 1999.

Schafer, Susan. *Tigers*. New York: Benchmark Books/Marshall Cavendish, 2001.

WEB SITES

5 Tigers: The Tiger Information Center http://www.5tigers.org

Enchanted Learning http://www.enchantedlearning.com/subjects/mammals/tiger

National Geographic.com Kids http://www.nationalgeographic.com/kids/creature_feature/0012/tigers.html

INDEX